The Ultimate ADALO APP Development Guide

By Daniel Melehi

New April 2025 Edition

Contents

Introduction

Welcome to **The Ultimate ADALO APP Development Guide**. This book is designed to provide you with a comprehensive and engaging roadmap for building fully functional applications using Adalo. From the very basics of no-code development, to advanced topics such as integrating external APIs and optimizing performance, this guide will equip you with the knowledge and confidence to bring your app ideas to life.

Adalo is a powerful platform that allows you to build mobile and web apps without the traditional complexities of programming. This approach removes many barriers faced by first-time creators and opens new possibilities for seasoned developers looking to speed up their workflow. Whether you're a complete beginner or an experienced professional exploring no-code tools, our chapters will walk you through every step of the process.

By the end of this guide, you'll understand how to plan your project, organize your app's structure, work with data, and deploy your finished product. Along the way, we'll share practical tips and useful insights that will help you address challenges, streamline your development, and create impressive results. We hope you find this journey as exciting and fulfilling as we do— let's get started on building amazing Adalo apps together!

Enjoy reading through the chapters, and get ready to transform your app ideas into reality.

Chapter 1: Introduction to Adalo and No-Code Development

No-code development has revolutionized the way applications are created by removing the need to write extensive lines of traditional code. Adalo, as one of the leading no-code platforms, offers intuitive tools, streamlined interfaces, and a robust ecosystem to help you bring your vision to life faster than ever.

1.1 UNDERSTANDING THE NO-CODE MOVEMENT

At its core, the no-code movement empowers people from all backgrounds to build functional software. Instead of diving into complex programming languages, you work with drag-and-drop components, pre-built templates, and visual workflows. This approach:

- **Broadens accessibility** – lowers entry barriers for aspiring app creators and entrepreneurs.
- **Simplifies development** – shortens the learning curve, letting you focus on what your app does rather than how it's coded.
- **Saves resources** – reduces the time and cost required for production builds.

1.2 THE EVOLUTION OF NO-CODE PLATFORMS

No-code platforms started as simple website builders but have blossomed into robust app creation solutions. Adalo sits at the forefront of this evolution, earning rapid adoption because of its powerful data handling, user-friendly interface, and growing community of creators.

1.3 WHY CHOOSE ADALO?

Adalo's appeal lies in its balance of simplicity and functionality. You can quickly design your app screens, set up navigation, and connect to databases without writing a single line of code. Once you've mastered basic concepts, you'll discover a range of advanced features, including integrations, custom workflows, and even marketplaces for plugins and templates. With Adalo, you have the flexibility to shape your project to your unique requirements while still enjoying the benefits of rapid development.

Chapter 2: Navigating the Adalo Dashboard

Once you've created an account on Adalo, you'll find yourself in a clean and intuitive dashboard. This central workspace is where your project management journey begins, providing you with the tools needed to oversee every aspect of your app.

2.1 DASHBOARD OVERVIEW

The Adalo dashboard is designed to streamline your workflow. You'll see a list of your existing projects, alongside buttons to create a new app or clone an existing one. The interface offers:

- **Project Cards** – a snapshot of each app you've built or are building.
- **Account Settings** – quick access to billing preferences, personal info, and subscription details.
- **Community Resources** – links to Adalo's forums, tutorial portals, and support helpdesk.

2.2 PROJECT SETTINGS AND MANAGEMENT

When you open a project, you'll reach the main editor where you create and modify your screens, data collections, and user flows. Key features include:

- **Preview Mode** – allows you to test your app in real-time.
- **Publish Settings** – prepares your app for deployment to various channels (e.g., web or mobile stores).
- **Team Collaboration** – lets you share the project with other collaborators for real-time teamwork.

2.3 NAVIGATIONAL TIPS

The Adalo dashboard's left-hand categories make it quick to hop between design elements, data structures, and app settings. By familiarizing yourself with this layout early, you'll save time and reduce confusion as your project grows. Stay organized by naming your components, screens, and data collections clearly and consistently.

Chapter 3: Setting Up Your App Structure

A solid blueprint paves the way for a smooth development process. Defining your app's structure ensures the finished product meets user needs and aligns with the project's goals. In this chapter, we'll explore core steps and best practices to create a strong foundation for your Adalo project.

3.1 DEFINING APP OBJECTIVES

The first step is to outline your app's purpose. Ask yourself:

- **Who** is my target audience?
- **What** core features solve the primary user pain points?
- **How** will the app be used (mobile, web, or both)?

Answering these questions keeps your design focused and helps you avoid feature creep.

3.2 VISUALIZING THE USER FLOW

Sketch out how users will navigate through your app's screens. A clear user flow chart helps you envision the layout of each screen and how they connect. This often includes:

- **Login and Registration**– for apps requiring user accounts.
- **Core Functionality Screens**– where key app actions occur (e.g., viewing products, booking services).
- **Profile or Settings Area**– for managing personal details or app preferences.

3.3 PLANNING AND SKETCHING LAYOUTS

Next, detail the visual structure for each screen. Start with simple wireframes either on paper or using a prototyping tool. Indicate where components like text fields, images, or buttons will reside, and think about how they'll respond on different devices. This exercise makes the move to Adalo's design editor much smoother, as you'll have a roadmap to follow.

Chapter 4: Key Concepts and Terminology

Before diving deeper into Adalo's functionalities, it's important to understand the basic principles and jargon used throughout the platform.

4.1 SCREENS

Screens are the fundamental building blocks of your Adalo app's user interface. They can represent anything from a sign-up page to a settings panel. Each screen houses components that work together to present data, collect user inputs, and display visuals.

4.2 COMPONENTS

Components are the individual elements you drag and drop onto a screen. They include text boxes, buttons, images, input fields, lists, and more. You can customize their styling, positioning, and behavior. The vast collection of components lets you build interactive interfaces with minimal effort.

4.3 DATA COLLECTIONS

Data collections are like databases within Adalo. They store information (such as user profiles, products, or orders) which can then be fetched and displayed in your app. Understanding how to create, organize, and link these collections is crucial for building dynamic applications.

4.4 ACTIONS AND WORKFLOWS

Adalo empowers you to define workflows through "Actions." These are the logical steps triggered by an event—such as tapping a button—that result in changes like creating a new record in a collection or navigating to a different screen. Actions make your app come to life by handling the behind-the-scenes logic.

4.5 EXTERNAL INTEGRATIONS

Adalo supports hooking into external services via APIs, giving you flexibility to pull in and push out data beyond your native collections. This can include integrating payment gateways, messaging services, or third-party tools that enhance your app's capabilities.

Chapter 5: Understanding Adalo Components

Adalo offers a wide range of built-in components that bring your app to life. From simple text elements to interactive lists and forms, each component is designed to save you development time while enhancing the user experience. Knowing how to configure and combine these resources effectively is crucial to building compelling apps that reflect your unique vision.

5.1 ESSENTIAL BUILT-IN COMPONENTS

Adalo's standard component library caters to the most common app functionalities. You'll find:

- **Text** – Ideal for headings, descriptions, and instructional content.

- **Buttons** – Trigger actions like navigating to another screen or submitting a form.
- **Forms** – Collect user inputs for everything from account setup to data collection.
- **Lists** – Display dynamic data from your collections, such as product listings or user directories.
- **Images** – Enhance your interface with visual elements that draw attention and convey information.

5.2 CONFIGURATION AND CUSTOMIZATION

Each component comes with various settings that let you personalize its size, color, font, and behavior. By fine-tuning these options, you can ensure consistent design across screens and tailor the user experience to specific use cases. Experiment with alignment, spacing, and styles to maintain a polished look and feel.

5.3 COMBINING COMPONENTS FOR ENHANCED INTERACTIVITY

A powerful feature of Adalo is the seamless way you can stack and layer components to create more sophisticated interfaces. Consider using lists that contain clickable buttons or embedding visual elements within forms. By mixing standard components creatively, you'll develop unique app sections without sacrificing usability.

Chapter 6: Working with Basic Screens

As you start constructing your Adalo app, basic screens form the backbone of your user journey. These screens present essential information, guide users through initial actions, and set the stage for more intricate functionalities down the line.

6.1 CREATING A NEW SCREEN

When you add a new screen, you choose its type—blank, list-focused, form-based, or a custom layout. Your selection dictates the default components that appear on the page. For instance, a list screen might automatically include a data-driven list, whereas a form screen could introduce input fields for user submissions.

6.2 SCREEN NAVIGATION AND FLOW

Screen navigation is pivotal in shaping how users interact with your app. Adalo's editor allows you to set "Link" actions on buttons or other interactive elements, which direct users to the desired screen. Thoughtful organization ensures that your audience effortlessly traverses the app, finding what they need with minimal clicks.

6.3 ESTABLISHING USER COMFORT

Basic screens often serve as introductions or landing spaces, so it's worthwhile to include clear headings, an intuitive layout, and short instructions where necessary. By welcoming users with a familiar structure, you boost their confidence and encourage continued exploration of your app's features.

Chapter 7: User Authentication and Accounts

For many apps, the ability to secure user profiles and personalize experiences is essential. Adalo's user authentication system offers robust, out-of-the-box features to handle sign-ups, logins, and password resets, all without needing to write a single line of code.

7.1 SETTING UP USER COLLECTIONS

Behind every registered account lies a "Users" collection, which stores personal information such as usernames, email addresses, and passwords. In Adalo, you can extend this default collection to include extra fields—like a profile photo or job title—to offer richer personalization options in your app.

7.2 REGISTRATION AND LOGIN FLOWS

Adalo provides pre-built authentication components that handle the sign-up and login process. Placing these components on designated screens allows new visitors to create an account or returning users to check in. Once authenticated, Adalo automatically recognizes the user's identity for subsequent interactions.

7.3 PASSWORD RECOVERY AND SECURITY

In cases of forgotten login details, you can integrate a password reset feature with minimal effort. This helps maintain user trust, as it offers a secure and straightforward path to regaining account access. Enhancing security by enforcing unique password rules or multi-factor authentication further ensures the safety of user data.

Chapter 8: Styling and Theming Your App

After establishing your app's structure and login flow, it's time to make it visually distinctive. Good design attracts users but also makes navigation smoother and more enjoyable, which is vital for long-term engagement.

8.1 COLORS, FONTS, AND BRAND IDENTITY

Adalo's design settings let you adjust global colors and typography. Selecting complementary hues and fonts that align with your branding visually ties all your screens together. Consistency creates a memorable impression, so choose guidelines that reflect your app's purpose and stick to them across various sections.

8.2 CREATING REUSABLE STYLES

Organization is the key to success when it comes to styling. Adalo enables you to define standardized color palettes and text styles that you can apply throughout your app. This practice saves time and simplifies future design tweaks—change a single style reference, and those edits cascade wherever that style is in use.

8.3 SCREEN LAYOUT TIPS

A well-structured layout directs attention to crucial actions while maintaining clear visual hierarchies. Experiment with spacing, icons, and background elements to highlight important information or clickable areas. Incorporating subtle accents— like shadows or bold text—can help guide the user's eye where you want it to go.

Chapter 9: Creating Responsive Layouts

In the modern app world, your users might access your product from multiple devices. Ensuring that every screen looks great and functions correctly on various screen sizes is a hallmark of a quality application.

9.1 THE IMPORTANCE OF RESPONSIVENESS

Responsive design ensures a seamless user experience, regardless of the device type or resolution. This approach not only enhances user satisfaction but also boosts accessibility, as people can comfortably interact with your app on phones, tablets, and desktops.

9.2 AUTOMATIC VS. MANUAL ADJUSTMENTS

Adalo simplifies responsiveness by automatically scaling and repositioning certain elements. However, it's still beneficial to manually review and refine your layout. Adjust component sizing, spacing, and alignment to guarantee that crucial parts of your interface remain visible and user-friendly.

9.3 TESTING ON MULTIPLE DEVICES

Before you finalize any design decisions, test your screens on a variety of devices and screen sizes. Adalo's preview mode offers quick checks, and you might also try external emulators for more comprehensive results. Taking time to test each screen layout under different conditions reduces surprises when your app goes live.

Chapter 10: Data Collections and Relationships

Adalo's data collections form the heart of your app, storing the information that powers dynamic content and personalized user experiences. By establishing the right relationships between those collections, you can streamline processes and reduce inconsistencies. Integrating these data structures effectively keeps your app running smoothly and makes your features more engaging.

10.1 STRUCTURING YOUR COLLECTIONS

When creating a collection, define the properties that best suit your app's requirements. Fields like text, number, and date are common, while more specialized ones (such as media or toggle fields) cover unique needs. Keep naming conventions consistent and organized—this simplifies troubleshooting and collaboration down the line.

10.2 COMMON RELATIONSHIP PATTERNS

Adalo supports different relationship types to help you link collections in meaningful ways:

- **One-to-One** – Ideal for pairing exclusive data, like a user with a single profile record.
- **One-to-Many** – Commonly seen when a single entry relates to multiple records in another collection (e.g., one author with many posts).
- **Many-to-Many** – Enables entries in both collections to reference multiple counterparts (e.g., users belonging to multiple groups).

Choosing the right relationship keeps your data manageable and ensures efficient retrieval.

10.3 OPTIMIZING DATA FOR PERFORMANCE

As your app grows, so does the volume of data you'll handle. Well-designed relationships reduce redundant information, making data lookups faster. Limiting nested references—where one collection links to another and back again—keeps your queries simpler. Adalo's built-in indexing also helps maintain performance by quickly filtering or sorting through larger datasets.

10.4 PRACTICAL TIPS FOR DATA MAINTENANCE

Regularly review your collections to ensure data integrity. Removing unused fields or archiving stale records keeps your database approachable. When you add new features, revisit your existing structures—sometimes minor adjustments to relationships or field types can improve overall app functionality.

Chapter 11: External Collections and APIs

While Adalo's native collections offer plenty of functionality, integrating external data sources opens the door to advanced customization. External collections and APIs enable your app to pull real-time information, automate tasks, and link with popular third-party services for more powerful features.

11.1 INTRODUCTION TO EXTERNAL INTEGRATIONS

External collections let you connect Adalo to external databases or APIs without storing data directly in your app. This is especially useful for syncing with services like Airtable, Google Sheets, or internal company systems. By accessing data remotely, you can extend your app's capabilities and keep large datasets in specialized repositories.

11.2 SETTING UP AN EXTERNAL COLLECTION

To create an external collection, you'll provide details like the API endpoint, authentication credentials, and how data should map to fields in Adalo. Follow these steps:

1. Identify a well-documented API or service.
2. Ensure you have appropriate read/write permissions.
3. Configure your collection's endpoints in Adalo's external data settings.
4. Link components (like lists) to this newly added external collection.

A successful connection means your app can display and manipulate data from the external source just like native collections.

11.3 MANAGING AUTHENTICATION AND SECURITY

APIs require secure interaction, typically handled by tokens, keys, or OAuth. Store these credentials in Adalo's settings to keep them protected and limit who can access them. Whenever possible, use encryption or SSL to safeguard sensitive data in transit.

11.4 PRACTICAL USE CASES

From pulling location-based data for a travel app, to displaying live inventory levels in a sales tool, external collections can supercharge your Adalo project. Look for widely-used APIs—like those for social media, mapping, or analytics services—and explore how they can enrich the functionality and user experience of your app.

Chapter 12: Payment Integration Basics

For apps centered on transactions—like online stores, subscription services, or donation platforms—accepting secure payments is paramount. By integrating payment functionality, you enable seamless checkout experiences that build trust and encourage conversions.

12.1 CHOOSING A PAYMENT PROVIDER

Several services specialize in processing online transactions, each with its own fee structure, geographic coverage, and technical requirements. Popular choices include Stripe, PayPal, and Braintree. Consider your target audience and budget when selecting a provider—some platforms may offer better rates for smaller-scale operations, while others offer robust international support.

12.2 PAYMENT SETUP CONSIDERATIONS

After picking a provider, you'll set up an account and obtain the relevant keys or tokens. In Adalo, integrate these credentials in the developer or plugin settings. Your payment flow typically includes:

- **Cart or Purchase Page** – Lists selected items or services plus pricing details.
- **Payment Processing** – Logs the transaction, verifies card details, and charges the user.
- **Confirmation Screen** – Informs the buyer that the payment was successful or flags issues if something went wrong.

12.3 ENSURING SECURITY AND COMPLIANCE

When handling credit card information, compliance with standards like PCI DSS is a must. Most reputable payment gateways automatically cover these regulations, but double-check that you're not storing sensitive data in non-secure fields. Transparency about how you handle user information fosters trust and signals professionalism.

Chapter 13: Building E-Commerce Features

With payments in place, it's time to step up your app's capabilities with full e-commerce functionality. Whether you're creating an online store, ticketing system, or marketplace, robust e-commerce features require careful planning of product catalogs, user interactions, and the entire purchase cycle.

13.1 SETTING UP A PRODUCT COLLECTION

Centralize your store items in a "Products" collection, listing details like titles, descriptions, prices, and images. Fields such as categories, inventory numbers, and ratings boost your users' browsing experience and keep product data organized. Adalo's relationship features help you link products with customers, wishlists, or order histories.

13.2 CREATING A COMPELLING SHOPPING FLOW

Craft a smooth path from product discovery to checkout. Common workflows include:

- **Product Browsing** – Lists or grids for item viewing, possibly filtered by brand or category.
- **Detailed Product Screens** – Provide specifications, pictures, and user reviews to entice purchases.

- **Shopping Cart** – Summarizes selected items with the option to modify quantity or remove products.
- **Checkout** – Integrates payment details and captures important delivery or contact information.

13.3 MANAGING ORDERS AND INVENTORY

When a customer makes a purchase, record the transaction in an "Orders" collection. This log tracks buyer info, order status, and shipping details. Connect it to your "Products" collection so inventory counts adjust automatically. Proper inventory management ensures users only see what's currently available, reducing frustration and overselling.

13.4 ENHANCING USER CONFIDENCE

E-commerce success often hinges on trust. Consider adding features like guest checkout, refund policies, or secure badges approved by your payment provider. Implement user-friendly design, transparent pricing, and easy return processes to keep shoppers coming back.

Chapter 14: Testing and Iterating Your App

Releasing an app without rigorous testing can lead to missed issues and user dissatisfaction. Iteration—refining your app through cycles of feedback and improvement—is equally crucial for delivering a steady, high-quality experience over time.

14.1 COMPREHENSIVE TESTING STRATEGIES

Before a public launch, perform multiple testing phases:

- **Functional Testing** – Confirm that each feature works as intended, from logging in to completing a purchase.
- **Usability Testing** – Involve actual or potential users to gauge user interface clarity, discover navigation pain points, and gather suggestions for improvement.
- **Performance Testing** – Identify slow loading screens or lag in data retrieval to maintain a smooth user experience.
- **Regression Testing** – Re-check existing functionality after adding new features, ensuring updates don't break prior components.

14.2 COLLECTING FEEDBACK

Engage early adopters to try your app and share their thoughts around design, performance, and missing features. Surveys, in-app chat, or email follow-ups work well to collect varied perspectives. Be open to critique—it often uncovers areas calling for improvement that you may have overlooked.

14.3 ITERATION AND UPDATES

Use feedback to guide refinements, focusing on solving the most critical pain points first. As you deploy updates, maintain versioning discipline so you can roll back if new changes introduce unexpected errors. Each iteration hones the user experience, helping your app stand out in a competitive market.

14.4 LAUNCHING WITH CONFIDENCE

Once major issues have been resolved and final testing is complete, prepare for an official release. By incorporating feedback loops and staying committed to incremental improvements, your Adalo app can evolve alongside user needs and remain relevant for the long haul.

Chapter 15: Advanced Workflows and Actions

In Adalo, actions are the backbone of dynamic user experiences—enabling everything from record creation to screen transitions. As your app grows in complexity, you'll likely need to orchestrate multiple actions and trigger them under specific conditions. This chapter explores advanced techniques for building powerful workflows that can significantly elevate your application's productivity and automation potential.

15.1 MULTI-STEP ACTIONS

One of the best ways to supercharge your interactions is to chain actions together. For instance, you might update a record, send an email notification, and then navigate to a confirmation screen—all triggered by a solitary button tap. By combining actions, you reduce manual steps for users and streamline complicated tasks into smoother, single-trigger workflows.

15.2 ACTION PRIORITIZATION AND ERROR HANDLING

When you create multi-step sequences, the order of execution becomes critical. Adalo processes actions in the sequence you set, so plan each event thoughtfully. Consider implementing fallback or error notifications—such as displaying an alert if one step fails—so you can capture mishaps, inform users, and preserve data integrity.

15.3 AUTOMATING TRIGGER RULES

Actions aren't limited to direct button clicks. Use timer-based triggers or link them to background processes to automate repetitive tasks, like sending periodic reminders or generating monthly reports. This flexibility ensures your app operates efficiently, providing updates or routine housekeeping without requiring consistent user input.

Chapter 16: Using Conditional Logic

Conditional logic refines your app's functionality by tailoring features to each user's specific context. With Adalo, you can display, hide, or modify elements based on criteria like user role, location, or data values—helping you craft interfaces that adapt in real time to reflect individual preferences and needs.

16.1 SHOW AND HIDE ELEMENTS

A common application of conditional logic is selectively revealing content. For example, you might show a "Manage Orders" button solely to administrators or hide certain form fields until a user opts in. This keeps interfaces uncluttered and ensures people only see options relevant to their situation.

16.2 DYNAMIC VISIBILITY WITH DATA

Adalo lets you associate component visibility with collection data. You can enable or disable elements based on numeric ranges, checkbox selections, or other record values. This technique is especially handy when implementing features like premium subscriptions—the system can block or unlock pages based on the user's subscription tier.

16.3 BRANCHING LOGIC FOR USER FLOWS

When designing interactive flows, condition-based branching can redirect users to different app screens or triggers. Suppose a form rating is above a certain threshold—Adalo can automatically route users to a success message, while lower scores might guide them to a survey for additional feedback. This flexibility not only improves the user journey but also ensures your app captures insights from diverse scenarios.

Chapter 17: Chat and Messaging Capabilities

Communication features are a powerful way to keep users engaged and foster community within your app. Whether you're building a support portal, social platform, or collaborative workspace, Adalo's chat and messaging tools simplify the process of integrating real-time discussions or private direct messaging.

17.1 CHAT INTERFACE ESSENTIALS

A basic chat interface typically consists of a message list, input field, and send button. Adalo's pre-built chat components handle storage of messages in a collection, linking them with users or channels. This foundation enables real-time conversation with minimal configuration. You can further personalize the appearance with custom fonts, colors, or system messages.

17.2 GROUP CHANNELS AND DIRECT MESSAGES

By leveraging many-to-many relationships, you can easily set up group channels where multiple users exchange messages simultaneously. For more private communication, you can design one-to-one chat functionality. Assign each conversation a unique identifier, ensuring messages remain private between the involved parties.

17.3 FILE SHARING AND RICH CONTENT

Enhance your messaging experience by supporting images, emojis, or other media. Storing and displaying attachments within your app fosters deeper user interactions. Consider file size limitations and user bandwidth needs—balancing visual engagement with optimal performance is crucial for a smooth chat experience.

Chapter 18: Push Notifications

Push notifications keep your audience informed about real-time updates—alerting them to new messages, feature launches, or special promotions. By implementing a reliable notification system, you encourage users to re-engage with your app, strengthening relationships and bolstering user retention over time.

18.1 SETTING UP A NOTIFICATION SERVICE

Adalo offers integrations with external notification providers like OneSignal to handle registration tokens and message sending. Once you've entered the necessary credentials, you can define triggers within your workflows. For instance, prompt an alert when someone receives a direct message or when a group chat topic is updated.

18.2 CUSTOMIZING NOTIFICATION CONTENT

Notifications perform best when they're timely and relevant. Incorporate placeholders for user names, message previews, or action prompts. The more personalized each notification, the greater its chance of sparking a meaningful user reaction— whether that's reading a new announcement or resuming an abandoned cart.

18.3 BEST PRACTICES FOR USER ENGAGEMENT

Strike a balance between too few and too many notifications. Inundating users with constant pings can lead to frustration or even uninstalls. Instead, focus notifications on the events that truly matter, like an urgent update or a personally relevant milestone. Provide an easily accessible settings page where users can customize their notification preferences.

Chapter 19: UI/UX Best Practices

While Adalo streamlines the technical aspects of app creation, thoughtful user interface (UI) and user experience (UX) design set your product apart. Crafting visually pleasing, intuitive layouts encourages prolonged engagement and respectful reviews.

19.1 CONSISTENCY AND CLARITY

Adhere to a uniform styling approach—use consistent font families, color schemes, and spacing throughout your screens. Set up predictable patterns, such as always placing action buttons in the same area, so users know where to find what they need without hesitation. Reducing visual chaos guides the user's attention to key features.

19.2 STREAMLINED NAVIGATION

Simple navigation ensures users can quickly locate essential features. Whether you choose a top bar, bottom tabs, or side menu, keep labels clear and easy to read. Implement relevant icons alongside text, and consider progressive disclosure—revealing more advanced options only when users dig deeper into the app's functionalities.

19.3 MICROINTERACTIONS AND FEEDBACK

Subtle animations, hover effects, or confirmation pop-ups let users know that their actions have been registered. For instance, a slight color change in a button click or a short success message after a form submission can provide a satisfying experience. These microinteractions prevent confusion and add a touch of personality to your app's design.

19.4 ACCESSIBILITY AND INCLUSIVITY

Designing for everyone includes catering to accessibility. Ensure text is legible for different levels of vision capabilities, use proper contrasting colors, and provide clear labeling for buttons or form fields to assist screen readers. Building inclusively broadens your audience and fosters genuine user satisfaction.

Chapter 20: Team Collaboration Essentials

When building an Adalo app as a group, effective collaboration can significantly boost workflow efficiency and overall app quality. By delegating tasks, sharing creative ideas, and maintaining organized communication channels, teams can harness each member's talents more effectively. Let's explore ways to manage collaborative Adalo projects while keeping everyone aligned on shared milestones.

20.1 INVITING AND MANAGING CONTRIBUTORS

Adalo's collaborative features let you add teammates to your project with different permission levels. Limiting editing rights to select individuals preserves consistency in the design and data structure. Clear role assignments—such as design lead or content manager—prevent overlap and promote smoother decision-making.

20.2 VERSIONING AND PROJECT ORGANIZATION

Staying organized with consistent naming and file structure is essential when multiple people work together. Decide on a naming convention for Collections, Screens, and Components at the beginning of the project. This practice ensures that everyone can quickly locate and update assets without confusion. Furthermore, backing up project versions regularly safeguards against conflicts in ongoing development.

20.3 COMMUNICATION AND FEEDBACK LOOPS

Routine check-ins—such as daily or weekly sync-up calls—help maintain visibility into each collaborator's progress and roadblocks. Here are a few tips for productive team interactions:

- **Share Transparent Updates** – Keep an open dialogue about completed tasks and upcoming objectives.
- **Leverage In-App Comments** – Use messaging or comment sections in Adalo for direct feedback on specific screens or components.
- **Store Documentation Centrally** – Whether it's best practices or design guidelines, a shared resource ensures new teammates learn the project quickly.

Chapter 21: Cloning and Reusing Templates

Efficiency is often rooted in not reinventing the wheel. In Adalo, "cloning" allows you to replicate existing apps and components to jumpstart new projects or reapply proven solutions to different use cases. This technique can drastically cut down development time, particularly for standard features like login pages or e-commerce layouts.

21.1 HOW CLONING WORKS

Cloning duplicates an entire application—complete with screens, collections, and actions. After cloning, you can adjust the copy to suit your new project. For instance, you might rename collections, restyle certain elements, or remove unneeded features while keeping the original app's core functionality intact.

21.2 CREATING YOUR OWN TEMPLATES

Over time, you might develop signature designs or app structures that you want to reuse. Adalo enables you to package these configurations as "templates," which can be:

- **Saved Internally** – Stored within your account for speedy project setup.
- **Shared Publicly** – Offered to the broader Adalo community to help others build their solutions.

21.3 BEST PRACTICES FOR TEMPLATE MAINTENANCE

When updating a template with new capabilities or bug fixes, document any significant changes. Clearly label your template versions so you can track which updates are included. This transparency helps you avoid confusion when multiple clones exist across different projects.

Chapter 22: Debugging Common Issues

Even the most carefully planned Adalo app can present unexpected glitches. Debugging is all about methodically identifying problems, determining their causes, and implementing fixes. By following organized troubleshooting steps, you'll save time and preserve app integrity.

22.1 IDENTIFYING SYMPTOMS AND POSSIBLE CAUSES

Signs of issues can range from blank screens to mismatched data or unresponsive buttons. Before delving deep into fixes, list visible symptoms to form hypotheses on potential triggers:

- **Is Data Not Displaying?** – Check if you've properly linked the collection or if permission settings are blocking retrieval.
- **Are Actions Failing?** – Verify that each step in your workflow is configured correctly and that no fields are left blank in required forms.
- **Is Navigation Improper?** – Confirm the correct screen link, ensuring you haven't accidentally set an action to the wrong destination.

22.2 A SYSTEMATIC DEBUGGING APPROACH

Step	Action
1	Reproduce the error consistently to confirm the scope of the problem.

2	Check app logs, if available, and inspect any relevant data fields or parameters.
3	Make small, controlled changes (like removing one action) to isolate the culprit variable.
4	Implement a fix and retest thoroughly across all relevant user scenarios.

22.3 LEVERAGING COMMUNITY AND SUPPORT

If you're stuck, consult Adalo's community forums or official support channels. Often, someone else has encountered a similar issue and found a solution. Sharing screenshots, error logs, or concise descriptions of your debugging steps helps others guide you to a quicker resolution.

Chapter 23: Integrating Third-Party Services

Adding external platforms to your Adalo app can elevate its capabilities significantly. Whether incorporating an email marketing tool, analytics system, or social media integration, third-party services let your app tap into broader ecosystems that enrich user experiences.

23.1 IDENTIFYING RELEVANT INTEGRATIONS

Focus on adding services that align with your app's core goals. For instance, if you're running an e-commerce store, you might link an email platform for automated newsletters. If community-building is key, consider single sign-on with major social networks to simplify registration. Choose integrations that truly amplify your app's purpose and suit your audience.

23.2 ESTABLISHING SECURE CONNECTIONS

Most third-party services require credentials—like API keys or tokens—to verify that your app is authorized. Safeguard these details by storing them securely within Adalo's integration settings. Always use secure (HTTPS) endpoints, and comply with any data privacy regulations the provider outlines.

23.3 MAPPING DATA SEAMLESSLY

Often, syncing user information or product details between Adalo and a third-party platform involves mapping of database fields. Double-check data formats—like name, email, or pricing—and use consistent naming conventions across systems. Test updates both ways to ensure everything merges accurately and on time.

Chapter 24: Gathering User Feedback

Feedback loops are fundamental to refining your Adalo app. By understanding how users interact with features, react to new updates, or struggle with certain tasks, you can plan enhancements that respond directly to their needs. Proactive feedback gathering is one of the best ways to insure continuous improvement.

24.1 IN-APP SURVEYS AND FORMS

One straightforward approach is embedding survey forms directly into your app. Consider short questionnaires or rating systems that appear after key user actions (like completing a purchase or saving a form). This method delivers immediate insights while minimizing user friction—especially if your questions are focused and concise.

24.2 ENCOURAGING OPEN DIALOGUE

Beyond structured surveys, offer users channels to voice suggestions or concerns freely:

- **Chat Support** – Enable real-time messaging for quick clarifications.

- **Feedback Screens** – Provide a dedicated screen where users can submit thoughts or complaints, possibly with attachments for screenshots.
- **Email or Social Media** – Encourage outreach through your preferred communication platform for more detailed discussions.

24.3 MINING ACTIONABLE INSIGHTS

The value of feedback lies in putting it to use:

- **Identify Trends** – If multiple people mention difficulty finding a feature, it's a sign to revise navigation or tutorials.
- **Prioritize Enhancements** – Weigh how many users will benefit from a suggestion versus the development effort required.
- **Close the Loop** – When implementing a user-driven change, let them know! Highlighting user-centered improvements fosters loyalty and engagement.

Chapter 25: Publishing Your Adalo App

Before your Adalo app can reach the hands of real users, you need to go through the publishing process. This stage involves finalizing your project settings, verifying that all links are functional, and adding finishing touches that elevate your creation from a prototype to a polished product.

25.1 REFINING YOUR APP FOR PUBLIC USE

Even if you've tested thoroughly before, it's wise to do one more pass just for final polishing. Inspect screen layouts, font sizes, images, and overall navigation flow. Make sure labels are easy to understand, and that each user action—like tapping a button or filling a form—works consistently. This attention to detail helps you avoid embarrassing errors post-launch.

25.2 USING ADALO'S PUBLISH SETTINGS

Adalo's built-in publish settings allow you to transition from editing mode to a live environment with a simple click. Choose whether you want your app accessible on the web, within a progressive web app (PWA), or through a native mobile build. During this step, confirm any custom domain settings, SSL certificates, and theme elements that reflect your unique branding.

25.3 PREPARING FOR ONGOING UPDATES

Publishing doesn't mean you're done—it just marks the beginning of your live product's life cycle. Plan a schedule or method for rolling out updates. Adalo's easy publishing system lets you release minor changes quickly, but always keep a backup strategy in case you need to revert to a previous version. Being prepared for rapid iteration can help you respond to feedback faster.

Chapter 26: App Store Submission Process

Once your Adalo app is polished and published as a native build, you may want to list it on major app marketplaces like Google Play and the Apple App Store. Following their specific rules and guidelines is crucial for a successful launch and to avoid rejections or delays.

26.1 CREATING DEVELOPER ACCOUNTS

Both Google and Apple require developers to register and pay an annual or one-time fee to host apps on their platforms. Setting up these accounts involves completing personal or business details, verifying identities, and agreeing to terms of service. Plan extra time for this process if you're registering for the first time, as approvals can take a few days.

26.2 MEETING STORE REQUIREMENTS

Each marketplace has specific content policies, design standards, and technical necessities. For example, Apple often emphasizes strict visual and performance criteria, while the Google Play Store might focus on security and device compatibility. Review guidelines for app icons, description metadata, privacy disclosures, and in-app purchase rules. Aligning with these requirements early helps you avoid multiple review cycles.

26.3 SUBMITTING FOR REVIEW AND MANAGING UPDATES

After uploading your build, the store's review process begins. This involves automated checks and possibly human reviews to ensure compliance with policies. If your app is rejected, you'll receive feedback detailing the reasons—use this as a guide to address issues and resubmit quickly. Once your app is approved, publish updates whenever you need by incrementing your build version, uploading new binaries, and responding to user reviews that appear in the store.

Chapter 27: Monetization and Subscription Models

Successful apps often explore revenue streams that fit user needs and business goals. Adalo helps you implement everything from one-time purchases to recurring subscriptions without heavy technical overhead.

27.1 CHOOSING THE RIGHT REVENUE STRATEGY

Your revenue model dictates how users perceive and engage with your offering. Options include:

- **Freemium** – Core functionality is free, with paid upgrades or premium features.
- **One-Time Purchases** – Customers pay once for full access, fitting single-purpose apps.
- **Subscription Plans** – Recurring charges for ongoing service, ideal for content updates or ongoing value.

Evaluate your target audience's expectations and willingness to pay to find a model that feels natural and profitable.

27.2 INTEGRATING PAYMENT GATEWAYS

Once you settle on a strategy, link your Adalo app to reliable payment processors. If you opt for native mobile monetization, be aware of in-app purchase guidelines from Google and Apple, which often take a commission and impose policy requirements. Navigating these details carefully helps prevent complications during store reviews.

27.3 MANAGING USER SUBSCRIPTIONS

Subscriptions require a robust system for billing cycles, renewals, and cancellations. Consider storing subscription status within your user collection to tailor your UI—like hiding premium pages for unsubscribed users. Routine checks, automated reminders, and straightforward cancellation processes ensure a positive reputation for your subscription model.

27.4 TRANSPARENCY AND COMPLIANCE

When handling payments, clarity fosters trust. Display clear metrics about charges, renewal dates, and usage limits. Also, follow regional data protection laws and payment industry standards to give users confidence that their sensitive information is secure. Transparency not only builds credibility but also helps you avoid legal troubles.

Chapter 28: Creating Multi-Language Apps

In our increasingly global market, supporting multiple languages can significantly expand your audience. Adalo makes it feasible to create multi-language apps by carefully organizing text elements, labels, and user-specific content so you can adapt seamlessly to different locales.

28.1 PLANNING FOR LOCALIZATION

Effective localization starts at the design stage. Decide which languages to offer based on your user demographics, and consider cultural nuances that may affect date formats or color interpretations. Keep interface text in separate files or collections where possible, so translations can be swapped in and out without disrupting your layout.

28.2 HANDLING DYNAMIC TRANSLATIONS

Leverage Adalo's data structure to store multiple language variants for each label or text snippet. For example, a "title" field might have English, Spanish, and French equivalents, with conditional logic to display the correct version based on user preference. This structure ensures minimal duplication of screens and a smoother user experience across languages.

28.3 SETTING UP LANGUAGE PREFERENCES

Provide a simple interface—like a dropdown menu—where users can select their desired language. Store their choice in their user profile or device settings. Once set, use conditional logic to render content exclusively in that language. This approach empowers each user with control over how they interact with your app, improving satisfaction.

Chapter 29: Scaling Your Adalo Projects

As your user base grows, your Adalo app must handle more traffic, larger data volumes, and increasingly complex feature requests. Proactive scaling strategies ensure you can meet the demand without compromising speed or reliability.

29.1 RECOGNIZING GROWTH TRIGGERS

Be attentive to early signs of strain, such as sluggish loading times, frequent error messages, or user feedback about instability. These signals often indicate your current infrastructure is nearing its capacity. Addressing them promptly helps you secure a positive reputation and avoid user attrition.

29.2 PERFORMANCE AND EFFICIENCY OPTIMIZATIONS

Adalo's hosting infrastructure is robust, but you can still refine your app to run more efficiently:

- **Streamline Collections** – Purge old data and archive unused records to improve query speeds.
- **Use Lists Wisely** – Limit the number of items that render on-screen by default, offering pagination or "load more" buttons.
- **Minimize Unnecessary Calls** – Combine or optimize external API requests wherever possible.

29.3 PREPARING FOR ENTERPRISE-LEVEL FEATURES

If your app evolves into an enterprise solution, consider additional capabilities like advanced user roles, single sign-on, and sophisticated reporting dashboards. Adalo's extensibility with APIs, plug-ins, or code embeds makes these expansions possible. Planning such features early prevents expensive rework later.

29.4 CONTINUOUS MONITORING AND IMPROVEMENT

Scaling isn't a one-time event. Regularly check analytics to see usage patterns, monitor server loads, and observe how your data collections grow. Establish a cycle where you introduce enhancements, collect feedback, and iterate on design. This mindset ensures your Adalo app remains stable, capable, and relevant no matter how large it grows.

Chapter 30: Performance Optimization

Ensuring your Adalo app runs smoothly is essential for retaining users and building credibility. Even if your application is feature-rich, poor performance can overshadow the benefits you've worked so hard to create. By employing a few best practices—spanning interface efficiency to real-time diagnostics—you'll keep users engaged and satisfied.

30.1 MINIMIZING RESOURCE-HEAVY COMPONENTS

One quick way to improve performance is to reduce or optimize components that consume large amounts of memory or processing power. Heavy imagery, numerous animations, or repeatedly running queries can slow your app's loading times. Whenever possible, compress large images, limit on-screen animations, and batch data requests to keep your interface responsive.

30.2 FINE-TUNING DATA EFFICIENCY

Review your data retrieval logic to ensure each query is purposeful. It might be tempting to load multiple collections at once, but consider filtering or showing key details, then loading additional data on demand. Pagination, lazy loading, and caching critical data in user devices all help ensure that your app delivers quick results without sacrificing depth.

30.3 MONITORING AND DIAGNOSTICS

Proactive monitoring lets you catch bottlenecks before they impact users. Implement analytics or third-party monitoring services to track load times and error frequencies for each screen. In Adalo, set up dashboards that display performance metrics, highlighting trends or spikes in real time. These insights guide where you should invest your optimization efforts next.

Chapter 31: Advanced API Integrations

Beyond basic data connections, advanced API integrations open new possibilities for your app—ranging from AI-based recommendations to secure transaction protocols. Successfully bridging these specialized routes requires careful planning, extended testing, and a solid understanding of each provider's documentation.

31.1 LEVERAGING SPECIALIZED ENDPOINTS

Many external services offer distinct endpoints for niche tasks, like retrieving batch analytics in a single call or orchestrating complex operations with fewer requests. Identify these specialized endpoints in the API docs and integrate them into Adalo's external collections or custom actions. This approach can streamline traffic—even performing multiple operations in one request—reducing overhead on your side.

31.2 TWO-WAY DATA EXCHANGE

Advanced integrations often involve sending updates back to the external service. For instance, an inventory system might need frequent notifications on product availability. Ensure you map each field carefully and follow strict protocols for data validation, security keys, and versioning. Document your data flows, so your team understands every path information can take between Adalo and the external source.

31.3 HANDLING API ERRORS AND RATE LIMITS

APIs can fail for various reasons—network downtime, exceeded rate limits, or invalid credentials. Implement graceful error handling that catches issues early and informs users of next steps. For high-volume use, watch for rate-limit warnings from the service provider and consider implementing retries with backoff timing. A robust error management system protects your app's stability and preserves user trust.

Chapter 32: Building Custom Forms and Wizards

Forms are more than just a place for filling in data—they can guide users through complex workflows, help them discover new features, or simplify the onboarding process. Custom forms and multi-step wizards can be designed in Adalo to reduce user overwhelm and increase successful submissions.

32.1 DESIGNING FLEXIBLE FORMS

Adalo's drag-and-drop environment makes form creation straightforward, but advanced layouts may require creative thinking. Consider structuring fields dynamically, such as only revealing additional details when a user selects a specific option. Maintaining a cohesive style across all form sections—colors, fonts, and instructions—elevates consistency and user confidence.

32.2 IMPLEMENTING MULTI-STEP WIZARDS

Wizards break large tasks into smaller, digestible pieces. Rather than asking users to complete a lengthy form, split it into logical steps. For example, separate personal info, account preferences, and payment details. Use clear progress indicators so users know how many steps remain. This strategy reduces cognitive load and helps keep users focused on one task at a time.

32.3 ADVANCED VALIDATION TECHNIQUES

Go beyond standard validation—like checking for required fields—by including conditional checks based on user input. For instance, if someone indicates they're located in a particular region, you might require an extra address line or state code.

Whenever a validation fails, display helpful, localized messages so users can quickly correct mistakes and move forward.

Chapter 33: Offline Features and Data Sync

Reliable internet connectivity isn't always guaranteed. Offering offline capabilities can significantly enhance user satisfaction, especially for those in areas of intermittent coverage and for time-sensitive tasks. With Adalo, you can architect systems that store data locally and seamlessly sync it when the user comes back online.

33.1 SETTING UP LOCAL STORAGE

Local storage ensures critical pieces of data remain accessible without a constant server connection. Depending on your app's complexity, you might cache lists, images, or entire user profiles. This helps your users continue essential functions—like viewing recent activity or drafting messages—even if their internet drops unexpectedly.

33.2 HANDLING SYNC CONFLICTS

When a user reconnects, your app needs to decide which version of data is correct: the local copy or the server's. Strategies include favoring the most recent edit, prompting the user to choose, or merging changes for collaborative entries. Whichever path you choose, document your approach to avoid confusion and keep data accurate.

33.3 MAXIMIZING OFFLINE USER EXPERIENCE

Even offline, your interface should remain informative. Provide clear indicators or icons that show offline status and outline which features remain available. If actions are pending, display a queue so users can see what will sync once connectivity resumes. These thoughtful design elements reassure users that your app is dependable—even off the grid.

Chapter 34: Data Privacy and Security

Data protection goes hand-in-hand with trust. Whether you're collecting email addresses or processing transactions, implementing stringent security standards and transparent privacy policies is crucial for user confidence and regulatory compliance.

34.1 SAFEGUARDING USER INFORMATION

Start by limiting data collection to only what is truly necessary. Less stored information means fewer vulnerabilities. Where possible, implement encryption—both at rest and in transit—to shield data from unauthorized access. Adalo's integrated security features can be enhanced with additional layers, such as password encryption workflows or third-party verification services.

34.2 COMPLIANCE AND LEGAL CONSIDERATIONS

Familiarize yourself with global and regional regulations like the General Data Protection Regulation (GDPR) or the California Consumer Privacy Act (CCPA). These rules dictate how you must collect, store, and handle personal information. Including a clear terms of service and privacy policy within your app can help you stay transparent about data management and mitigate legal risks.

34.3 RESPONDING TO SECURITY THREATS

Even with robust precautions, threats may emerge. Regularly update your Adalo components, particularly if security patches are released. In the event of a data breach or phishing attempt, have an incident response plan in place. Promptly notifying affected users, investigating the cause, and fixing vulnerabilities demonstrates accountability and upholds brand integrity.

Chapter 35: Advanced Filtering and Sorting

Sophisticated filtering and sorting capabilities provide users with more control over how they view data. By giving people the power to fine-tune lists, tables, or galleries to their needs, you create a more interactive and personalized experience. This chapter explores methods to empower users with flexible search tools, comprehensive filters, and intelligent sorting features.

35.1 IMPLEMENTING MULTI-CONDITION FILTERS

Sometimes, users need to filter through data collections based on multiple criteria—such as date ranges, categories, or textual searches. To achieve this, you can stack various filter components in a single interface, each responsible for refining specific parameters. Consider offering preset filters for beginners while allowing more advanced users to configure several conditions at once. This layering of filters provides deeper insights into the data without overwhelming the interface.

35.2 ENABLING REAL-TIME QUERYING

Waiting for data to load after every filter change can frustrate users, especially if your app features numerous records. Real-time querying addresses this issue by automatically updating lists as users apply or remove filters. This approach relies on efficient data handling within Adalo, ensuring that changes in input fields or toggles reflect instantly in the displayed results—making data exploration seamless.

35.3 USER-DEFINED SAVED SEARCHES

For apps storing large or frequently updated collections, offering saved searches can save time and boost convenience. Users can name and store their preferred sets of filter conditions, then recall them later with a single click. Some may want to bookmark popular items, while others maintain different configurations for future comparisons. Including a dedicated section for personalizing search parameters enhances your app's usability and fosters deeper engagement.

35.4 SORTING AND RANKING TECHNIQUES

Simple alphabetical or date-based sorting is a great start, but advanced apps often require more nuanced ranking options. You might integrate user ratings, popularity scores, or algorithmic methods that elevate certain entries above others. Clearly label each sortable column or category and allow toggling between ascending/descending orders. Comprehensive sorting maintains transparency by showing users exactly how their data is organized.

Chapter 36: Membership and Restricted Content

Different user groups often require tailored access to functionalities and content. Membership systems allow you to cultivate exclusivity, monetize premium features, and manage diverse user types. In this chapter, we'll delve into setting up robust membership tiers and controlling who can see or interact with specific parts of your app.

36.1 CRAFTING MEMBERSHIP TIERS

Membership tiers classify users under categories like free, basic, or premium access. Each level can unlock a distinct set of features, sections, or benefits. You can store this tier information in a "Membership" field within the user collection. By associating user accounts with these levels, your app can determine what content or pages to show upon login. Beyond revenue generation, membership tiers can also streamline content moderation, ensuring that only the right audience accesses certain features.

36.2 CONTROLLING PAGE VISIBILITY

Adalo's conditional logic helps limit who can view specific pages. For example, if a member does not meet certain criteria—like having a paid subscription—redirect them to an upgrade prompt or alternative page. This approach allows you to maintain a seamless user journey while still safeguarding exclusive sections of your app. Make sure your app communicates any restrictions clearly, reducing confusion and supporting a positive user experience.

36.3 PASSWORD-PROTECTED CONTENT

While memberships are typically tied to user roles, you may also need additional security measures for sensitive data. Some apps benefit from standalone password-guarded sections, particularly if they contain confidential documents or personal information. Integrating password prompts within restricted sections gives you a second layer of defense, ensuring that only truly authorized individuals can proceed.

36.4 TIER UPGRADES AND DOWNGRADES

Over time, users may wish to switch between tiers—upgrading from basic to premium, for instance. Provide simple UI flows for these transitions, updating the user's tier status in real time. Automate the changes to any billing or subscription details, ensuring consistency across your entire platform. Tracking these shifts can also inform decision-making about which benefits users value the most, guiding future updates and improvements.

Chapter 37: Scheduling and Automating Tasks

Automating routine tasks can save time, reduce human error, and keep your app running smoothly around the clock. By leveraging scheduled functions or connecting with external services, you can have repetitive processes occur reliably in the background. This chapter tackles scheduling fundamentals and best practices for creating efficient automated workflows.

37.1 TRIGGERS AND TIMERS

The first step to automation is deciding how jobs will be triggered. If a specific time of day always kicks off an action—like sending reminders every Monday morning—you can integrate with triggers from external workflow platforms (e.g., Zapier, Make) or employ custom code solutions. Ensure your chosen approach can handle robust scheduling options to accommodate unique business needs, including daily, weekly, or monthly intervals.

37.2 BACKGROUND DATA PROCESSING

Sometimes, bulky data operations—like recalculating analytics or archiving old records—should run behind the scenes without hindering real-time performance. You can automate these tasks using external workflows or specialized plugins that periodically call your Adalo database, update entries, or generate reports. Designing these processes carefully avoids excessive system strain and keeps your front-end users focused on the app's core features.

37.3 NOTIFICATIONS AND ALERTS

Scheduled tasks often include sending out emails, push notifications, or SMS messages. For instance, you might remind users their subscription is about to expire or prompt them to revisit abandoned cart items. Timing is key—sending relevant messages at precisely the right moment can significantly boost engagement and trust in your platform. Always offer an "opt-out" mechanism to stay compliant with messaging regulations and respect user privacy.

37.4 MONITORING AUTOMATED FLOWS

Relying on automated schedules shouldn't mean ignoring them. Regularly review logs and track success or failure rates of each procedure. By spotting patterns— like repeated errors at certain times—you can identify root causes and refine your approach. Keeping a close eye on automation health ensures stable performance, making your Adalo app more reliable for users who depend on timely updates.

Chapter 38: Personalizing User Experiences

No two users share the exact same preferences, backgrounds, or goals, so why should their app experiences be identical? Personalization involves tailoring content, layouts, and features based on each individual's behavior or profile. This level of customization can boost engagement, loyalty, and satisfaction with your product.

38.1 ADAPTIVE CONTENT STRATEGY

Start by capturing a few essential data points from each user, such as their interests or daily habits. Use these insights to display relevant content—like recommended articles or curated product lists—directly on their home screen. The more specific you can be, the more valued and understood users will feel. Over time, expand this approach with additional nuances, including location-based suggestions or time-based updates.

38.2 DYNAMIC LAYOUTS

Layout personalization focuses on optimizing the interface for each user. You could allow them to rearrange widgets or choose which sections appear most prominently in their dashboard. By offering simple drag-and-drop or toggle mechanisms, your app feels more like a tailored environment rather than a one-size-fits-all product. This approach also turns casual users into active participants in shaping their in-app journey.

38.3 CUSTOM ONBOARDING PATHS

When someone opens your app for the first time, a contextual onboarding flow can make a transformative first impression. Rather than offering the same tour to everyone, you can adapt your tutorial screens based on user-provided data—such as expertise level or reason for downloading the app. Short, personalized guidance fosters confidence and helps new users find immediate value in your product.

38.4 ONGOING BEHAVIORAL TRACKING

To deepen personalization, track patterns in how users actually engage with features. If a certain topic earns repeat visits, highlight similar suggestions. Conversely, if someone repeatedly skips a section, you might adjust or hide it from their layout. This feedback loop ensures your app continually adapts, reflecting real user habits instead of assumptions made at the outset.

Chapter 39: Integrating Analytics Tools

Informed decisions stem from valid data. Where are your users dropping off? Which screens receive the most engagement? By integrating analytics tools, you can measure these metrics and many more, transforming raw numbers into actionable insights.

This chapter illustrates how to connect robust analytics platforms with your Adalo app and interpret the results effectively.

39.1 SELECTING THE RIGHT ANALYTICS PLATFORM

From universal options like Google Analytics to specialized platforms such as Amplitude or Mixpanel, the choice depends on your project's needs. Some services emphasize funnels and retention, while others focus on real-time dashboards or advanced segmentation. Evaluate your goals—like understanding user behavior or fine-tuning conversions—to narrow down the options. Look for tools that match your required granularity and align with your budget.

39.2 EMBEDDING TRACKING SCRIPTS

Many analytics solutions rely on small snippets of code placed within your app or web build. In Adalo, you can integrate these scripts via custom actions or embedded components. Ensure your tracking calls trigger at the right moments—page views, button clicks, or form submissions—so you capture meaningful data. Verify the setup using the analytics platform's diagnostics, checking that events register accurately in reports.

39.3 DEFINING KEY PERFORMANCE INDICATORS (KPIS)

Before diving into raw data, clarify the metrics that matter most. Are you focused on conversion rates, average session duration, or monthly active users? Pinpoint these KPIs in your analytics dashboard so you can quickly gauge whether your app meets benchmarks or lags behind. By focusing on select KPIs, you avoid drowning in excessive data and keep your team aligned on the metrics tied to success.

39.4 INTERPRETING DATA AND TAKING ACTION

Collecting analytics is only the first step; turning them into concrete improvements is what truly counts. Organize regular reviews of key metrics and identify patterns—like peak usage times or user drop-off points. Propose evidence-based refinements, then monitor subsequent changes in data to validate your strategy. This ongoing, analytics-driven cycle helps your Adalo app evolve in ways that consistently meet user needs and achieve measurable milestones.

Chapter 40: Custom Components and Plugins

As your app ideas grow more ambitious, you may find that the built-in Adalo components, while powerful, aren't enough to achieve every goal. That's where custom components and plugins come into play. By extending the platform's native capabilities, you can tap into unique features, external libraries, or specialized user interactions that distinguish your app from the crowd. Whether you want to render complex charts, integrate device-specific hardware, or incorporate specialized animations, custom solutions allow you to transform creative concepts into seamless experiences.

40.1 UNDERSTANDING THE CUSTOM DEVELOPMENT WORKFLOW

Before building a custom component, outline its purpose and target functionality. Check component development guides and plan out the data inputs, outputs, and styles you'll need to manage. A clear roadmap simplifies the actual coding process and minimizes guesswork. Once you've built a prototype, test it against a variety of use cases to confirm it behaves properly across different screens, devices, or user flows.

40.2 EMPLOYING THE ADALO COMPONENT TOOLKIT

Adalo's Component Toolkit provides structure for creating and deploying custom elements. Utilizing this toolkit, you can code your feature in JavaScript and React, wrap it in a package, and import it into Adalo's environment. Throughout development, keep performance in mind—inefficient or unoptimized code can slow your application. Also, ensure your styling remains consistent with the rest of your brand and that any customization options are intuitive for design and editing purposes.

40.3 PLUGIN ARCHITECTURE AND DISTRIBUTION

Plugins act as self-contained modules that can be quickly incorporated into different apps. If your custom functionality could benefit others—like a specialized payment app or a messaging interface—consider packaging it as a plugin for easier distribution. Proper versioning, with clear release notes and documentation, makes it simpler for collaborators or customers to integrate your work into their own projects. If you plan to make the plugin public, test extensively to cover a wide range of user scenarios and minimize potential conflicts with other components.

40.4 BEST PRACTICES FOR MAINTENANCE

Over time, new Adalo releases and changes in web technologies may affect your custom components. Set up a maintenance schedule to review performance, fix reported bugs, and update compatibility. Keep an open feedback loop with your team or user community—any issues they experience can be patched quickly if you have a clear process for version control and documentation. In this way, your custom solutions continue to evolve in line with both Adalo's own advancements and your audience's shifting needs.

Chapter 41: Leveraging the Adalo Marketplace

As you work on sophisticated apps, you'll likely discover an impressive range of ready-made resources on the Adalo Marketplace. From pre-built components to fully-fledged templates, the marketplace can dramatically speed up your workflow. This chapter will show you how to find hidden gems and integrate them effectively into your project so you can spend less time reinventing the wheel and more time focusing on features that set your app apart.

41.1 NAVIGATING AVAILABLE RESOURCES

Open the Adalo Marketplace from your dashboard and explore the categories that match your development goals—like user interface elements, data handling upgrades, or specialized page templates. Each listing provides a concise overview, images, and user ratings. Read through feedback and check for compatibility notes to see if the component or template will suit your particular needs. Once you decide on an item, quickly add it to your project for immediate use.

41.2 EVALUATING QUALITY AND RELIABILITY

Not all marketplace items are created equal. Before finalizing your choice, check whether the developer regularly updates their submission, responds to questions, and maintains clear documentation. A high rating and positive reviews often indicate that other users have tested it in real-world scenarios. It's also wise to make a backup of your project before installing newly published or unverified components, protecting your main build in case compatibility issues emerge.

41.3 CONTRIBUTING TO THE MARKETPLACE

If you develop a reusable solution—for instance, a polished chat interface or a specialized login flow—sharing it on the

Marketplace can earn recognition and even revenue. Provide thorough instructions, release notes, and any relevant screenshots or demos to showcase your work. Make it easy for others to adopt by offering ample guidance, including example data or usage tips. Over time, your contributions can strengthen your personal brand and foster a sense of community among Adalo developers.

41.4 KEEPING YOUR MARKETPLACE ASSETS CURRENT

When you add someone else's template or component, watch for any updates or bug fixes. Regularly check the Marketplace notifications and handle upgrades carefully to avoid breaking changes in your live app. If you're a contributor, remain responsive to support requests and update your listing whenever you fix a bug or add a feature. This level of attention benefits end users, ensures your product remains in high demand, and helps preserve the overall ecosystem's quality.

Chapter 42: Setting Up White-Label Solutions

White-labeling involves customizing the appearance, branding, and even functionality of an app so that it can be resold or delivered under another entity's identity. This approach is particularly useful for agencies or freelancers who create Adalo apps on behalf of multiple clients. By seamlessly masking any third-party platform references, you provide a professional, cohesive product that resonates with each client's brand guidelines.

42.1 BRANDING ESSENTIALS

Begin by gathering the client's logo, color palette, fonts, and key messaging. Replace any default Adalo visuals or placeholders with these custom assets. Pay attention to every corner of the interface, from login screens to error messages, to maintain a uniform look. In some cases, you may even rename system labels or notifications to strengthen brand authenticity. Make sure your design choices align with accessibility standards, preserving readability and usability across devices.

42.2 CUSTOM DOMAINS AND URLS

Hosting your app on a personalized domain (e.g., app.clientname.com) further reinforces the white-label experience. Configure domain settings, apply SSL certificates for data protection, and confirm that all links or media references maintain the consistent brand identity. This next-level customization cements the perception that the client owns the product, fostering trust among their end users.

42.3 MANAGING MULTIPLE CLIENTS

If you serve more than one client, a scalable approach becomes crucial. Adalo's editor can help you clone or template widely used layouts—like e-commerce or membership dashboards—and re-skin them for each new customer. Keep a standardized project folder structure, naming convention, and documentation so adjustments can be made smoothly. Speed and efficiency improve, letting you focus on adding genuinely innovative features rather than repeating the basics each time.

42.4 QUALITY ASSURANCE AND HANDOVER

Once your white-label solution is complete, perform rigorous tests under the client's brand guidelines. Look for any leftover references or placeholders that might hint at a separate framework. Conduct a thorough audit, including load tests, user journey simulations, and cross-device checks. Finally, present the finished product with a straightforward handover process or ongoing maintenance contract, depending on the agreement, ensuring the client has all they need to launch confidently.

Chapter 43: Working with Complex Data Structures

Large-scale apps often need sophisticated data models to handle layered information sets—think nested categories, multi-step workflows, or compound relationships between user roles and resources. Mastering the art of structuring complex data ensures your Adalo project remains flexible, swift, and easy to maintain, even as features multiply.

43.1 ADVANCED JOINS AND SUB-COLLECTIONS

Simple one-to-many or many-to-many relationships might not always suffice for complicated requirements. Sub-collections, also known as nested data structures, help store grouped or hierarchical information in a more logical format. For instance, a task management app might assign sub-tasks to main tasks, each with its own set of properties like deadlines or attachments. Plan these nesting levels carefully—overly intricate relationships can bloat your app's complexity and hamper performance.

43.2 MULTI-STEP DATA PROCESSING

When data flows through multiple states—like a request that transforms into an invoice, then transitions to a completed order—define each "stage" in a dedicated collection or field. This approach improves traceability and allows you to process data at each step. Set up automated actions for transitions, verifying that each record is updated accurately. To avoid confusion, keep naming schemes consistent across all stages.

43.3 SEGMENTING FOR ANALYTICS AND REPORTING

Complex data often fuels in-depth reports—like daily user activity logs or turnover statistics. Aggregate only the fields necessary for analytics, perhaps by creating specialized collections dedicated to storing daily or monthly summaries. Strategically segmenting your data lets you pinpoint bottlenecks and trends while preventing the main collections from being overwhelmed with historical or repetitive records.

43.4 MAINTAINING PERFORMANT QUERIES

Even with intricate data structures, your app should swiftly retrieve and display relevant information. Minimize repeated lookups by caching or batching requests, and carefully consider which fields truly need to be fetched in list views. Keep an eye on slow-running screens—this could signal suboptimal relationships or unfiltered queries. A thoughtful combination of indexing, filtering, and targeted collection usage can keep your app agile and well-organized.

Chapter 44: Handling User Roles and Permissions

In an app that caters to assorted user groups—like customers, managers, or administrators—role-based permissions guarantee that each individual only sees and interacts with data and features they're authorized to access. Properly implementing and managing user roles can safeguard your application from accidental misuse while opening up specialized utility for higher-tier users.

44.1 DEFINING YOUR ROLE HIERARCHY

Start by mapping out which roles need to exist within your app and how they relate to each other. A typical hierarchy might include "Regular Users" at the foundation, "Editors" who can modify content, and "Admins" with full oversight. Plan precisely which actions each group can perform—like editing, approving, or deleting records. This clarity up front prevents confusion when coding or applying permissions.

44.2 CREATING CONDITIONAL ACCESS

Adalo's conditional logic engine allows you to define when a page or component is visible based on the logged-in user's role. For instance, an admin panel might appear only if a user's "role" field equals "Admin." Alternatively, you can limit certain forms to read-only mode unless the person has permission to edit. This granular approach weaves security checks directly into the user experience without introducing cumbersome complexity.

44.3 PROTECTING SENSITIVE DATA

In addition to gating screens, confirm that private information remains hidden at the database level. Even if a screen is invisible, savvy users might try to access the data in other ways—via direct links or unauthorized requests. Implement server-side rules or carefully design your collections so only permissible queries succeed. This layered approach ensures robust security, especially when storing personal user details or confidential business metrics.

44.4 AUDITING AND ALERTS

Once roles and permissions are active, consider setting up an audit trail system. Tracking which user performed certain updates or accessed restricted screens can help you investigate issues or suspicious behavior. For high-stakes operations—like deleting records or confirming financial transactions—send admins real-time notifications or alerts. An open monitoring process both deters malicious actions and reassures users that your platform values transparency and accountability.

Chapter 45: Version Control and Release Cycles

Managing your Adalo app's evolution in an organized manner helps you keep track of changes, maintain stability, and smoothly introduce new features. While software developers traditionally rely on systems like Git for version control, you can still establish effective release processes within Adalo. By structuring your workflow, documenting every stage, and testing systematically, you'll be better equipped to handle whatever surprises come your way.

45.1 ESTABLISHING VERSIONING GUIDELINES

Even though Adalo doesn't inherently integrate with traditional versioning software, you can create a manageable process by defining rules for each update. For instance, decide if you will label a minor design tweak as "1.1" while reserving major releases—those with structural overhauls or new functionality—for bigger increments like "2.0." This attention to labeling clarifies the nature of your changes and sets expectations for team members and users alike.

45.2 STAGING, TESTING, AND PRODUCTION

Developing a structured environment—such as "staging" for experimental builds before going "live"—helps you isolate bugs and refine new features. In Adalo, you might maintain a cloned project that mirrors your primary application. Test new ideas thoroughly in this staging environment, ensuring minimal disruption for your main user base. Once tested, you can confidently roll out changes to the live, production app, knowing that each feature has passed through a quality review.

45.3 PLANNING A RELIABLE RELEASE CYCLE

Adopt a predictable release cycle—monthly, bi-weekly, or quarterly—so that your team can plan tasks and your users have a clear timeline. Coordinate with collaborators on which features or fixes to include in each cycle. Keep a changelog that documents each new capability or fix, providing transparency and enabling quicker troubleshooting if any issues surface. This approach cultivates user trust, as people can anticipate how and when the app will evolve.

Chapter 46: Collaborating with Clients

When building Adalo apps for clients—whether small businesses, nonprofits, or large enterprises—honing effective collaboration skills is crucial. Maintaining open communication, presenting clear timelines, and accommodating feedback ensure both parties remain on the same page and that the final product meets expectations.

46.1 DEFINING PROJECT OBJECTIVES AND SCOPE

Begin your client relationship by clarifying the project's vision and boundaries. Prepare questionnaires or discovery sessions to learn what the client hopes to achieve, their budget constraints, and any non-negotiable requirements. Use this information to form a detailed project scope document, which you can refer back to whenever questions arise or priorities shift. This shared reference keeps misunderstandings to a minimum and paves the way for a smooth workflow.

46.2 DEMONSTRATING PROGRESS WITH PROTOTYPES

One of Adalo's strengths lies in its rapid app-building capabilities, which facilitate quick mockups or prototypes. Developing rough versions of core features early on helps clients visualize the final product and provide feedback. Encourage iterative reviews at key milestones, such as after major design updates or when adding complex functionality. This approach prevents last-minute changes by catching issues early on, saving both time and resources.

46.3 STREAMLINING FEEDBACK AND REVISIONS

Clients often have busy schedules, so make it easy to contribute ideas and suggestions. You could set up shared documents for comments, use Adalo's collaboration tools, or schedule regular video calls. Keep a running list of requested changes, marking each as "in progress" or "completed." By clearly tracking revisions, you minimize confusion, maintain a healthy working relationship, and deliver an app that precisely meets the client's needs.

Chapter 47: Post-Launch Maintenance

Launching an Adalo app is the culmination of countless hours of design, development, and testing. Yet the journey doesn't end once it's available to users. Maintaining, updating, and refining your app after launch helps ensure that users remain satisfied, engagement stays positive, and potential issues get resolved swiftly.

47.1 MONITORING EARLY PERFORMANCE

Shortly after launch, keep an eye on analytics or user feedback channels. Look out for unexpected drops in performance, unusual error reports, or recurring questions about specific features. Rapidly addressing any showstopper bugs or usability hurdles prevents negative first impressions from spreading. Proactive monitoring not only safeguards your reputation but also sets the stage for smoother long-term upkeep.

47.2 IMPLEMENTING SMALL-SCALE UPDATES

Even the best-planned app may require adjustments once real users begin interacting with it. Minor updates—such as text edits, color changes, or quick bug fixes—can go live promptly without waiting for a major release cycle. By refining your product based on real-world insights, you continually enhance the experience and reassure users that their feedback matters.

47.3 PLANNING FUTURE ENHANCEMENTS

As your app evolves, keep track of feature requests or market trends that could shape its trajectory. Distinguish between "nice-to-have" ideas and must-have improvements to maintain focus. Regularly consult your roadmap and prioritize enhancements that align with user needs and your business model. Scheduling these feature additions in phases ensures each revision is well-executed and tested before going live.

Chapter 48: User Retention Techniques

Acquiring new users is important, but keeping existing users engaged can be even more crucial to an app's ongoing success. By implementing thoughtful retention strategies—like personalized content and incentive systems—you can inspire long-term loyalty, minimize churn, and boost overall satisfaction.

48.1 REWARDING ENGAGEMENT

Features like loyalty points, achievement badges, or milestone celebrations motivate users to continue interacting with your app. These rewards don't need to be expensive or flashy—sometimes simple acknowledgments or subtle recognition can spark enthusiasm. If users feel valued for their continued engagement, they are more likely to explore fresh offerings or recommend your platform to others.

48.2 ACTIVE FEATURE REMINDERS

Push notifications and email reminders are powerful tools for gently prompting users to revisit your app. Highlight newly added functionalities, share exclusive promotions, or encourage them to complete an incomplete task. Tailoring messages to individual preferences increases the likelihood of re-engagement, striking a balance between being helpful and avoiding spam.

48.3 CULTIVATING COMMUNITY ELEMENTS

Introducing ways for users to interact with each other—through forums, user groups, or social media integrations—can foster a sense of belonging. When people form relationships around a shared app, it becomes more than just a tool; it transforms into part of their routine. Moderating and nurturing these communities to keep discussions respectful and valuable further strengthens user attachment and reduces abandonment.

Chapter 49: Marketing Your Adalo App

Even an exquisitely designed app can flounder without effective promotion. Marketing is the bridge between your creation and its intended audience, spanning everything from app store optimization to engaging social media strategies. Crafted thoughtfully, these tactics will generate buzz, expand your user base, and position your app to meet (or exceed) its goals.

49.1 CRAFTING A MARKETING ROADMAP

Start by identifying your target audience and clarifying the objectives for your marketing campaigns—whether that's driving app installs, boosting in-app purchases, or increasing brand awareness. Define the message you want your app to convey, be it convenience, affordability, or innovation. A solid roadmap focuses on concrete goals, timelines, and budget allocations, ensuring you can measure every marketing effort's impact.

49.2 UTILIZING MULTIPLE CHANNELS

People discover apps in myriad ways, so consider advertising across several touchpoints. Leverage social platforms like Instagram or LinkedIn for targeted ads, run email campaigns to a curated list, or establish partnerships with influencers relevant to your niche. Consistency is paramount—stick to a uniform tone, style, and branding identity regardless of which channel you're using. Users interacting with your content in different places should always experience the same key message.

49.3 MEASURING RESULTS AND ADAPTING

Once your campaigns are active, track metrics like click-through rates, conversion percentages, and usage durations. Studying these numbers reveals which methods succeed and which underperform, guiding you in refining your marketing plan. For instance, if you notice a spike in downloads but limited user retention, you might improve your onboarding funnel or focus on a different segment of the market. Evolving in response to data ensures your efforts remain both relevant and beneficial to the growth of your Adalo app.

Chapter 50: Continuous Improvement Strategies

Building an Adalo app is an evolving process. Whether you're looking to refine existing features or drive innovation, adopting a mindset of continuous improvement ensures your product remains current and user-focused. In this chapter, we'll explore techniques for sustaining momentum, incorporating ongoing feedback, and strategically responding to changes in technology and user expectations.

50.1 EMBRACING ITERATIVE DEVELOPMENT

Continuous improvement thrives on iteration—small cycles of development, testing, and review. By breaking larger initiatives into manageable phases, you can release new capabilities faster, collect real user input, and align updates closely with what your audience genuinely needs. This approach helps you create focused improvements, detect early mistakes, and pivot more efficiently when necessary.

50.2 LEVERAGING INSIGHTS FROM USER BEHAVIOR

Data-backed decisions lead to sharper iterations. Monitor analytics pointing to features with high engagement or areas where users frequently drop off. Add user feedback loops—like polls or rating prompts within the app—to gather continuous input. This steady inflow of data shapes your roadmaps, ensures improvements target real-life challenges, and fosters a sense of community-driven development.

50.3 REGULAR REVIEW AND AUDITING

Plan a periodic audit—monthly, quarterly, or annually—where you assess your Adalo app's design, performance, and architecture. Look for areas requiring code optimization or layout adjustments. Keeping track of improvements over time fosters better documentation and helps you avoid accumulating technical debt. Establishing a culture of regular review elevates your app's overall quality as it matures.

50.4 BALANCING INNOVATION WITH STABILITY

While continuous improvement encourages experimentation, it's also vital to maintain a stable foundation. Prioritize high-impact enhancements that can easily integrate without disrupting existing features. If you choose to try new technologies or design patterns, test them thoroughly in a staging environment before shifting to production. A well-balanced approach preserves reliability while still propelling your app forward.

Chapter 51: Extending Adalo with Code Embeds

Adalo's no-code framework is robust, but you may sometimes want to push boundaries even further. Code embeds offer the flexibility to insert custom scripts or interactive elements right into your Adalo app. By combining drag-and-drop simplicity with minimal coding, you can enhance user experiences or incorporate highly specific functionalities that go beyond Adalo's built-in components.

51.1 IDENTIFYING USE CASES FOR CUSTOM CODE

You may need code embeds when the existing component library doesn't quite match a desired feature—like a specialized slider, a unique menu animation, or an embeddable external widget. Each scenario should have a clear purpose: perhaps you want to present data from an external source or run a client-side calculation that Adalo's native tools can't handle on their own.

51.2 EMBEDDING SCRIPTS RESPONSIBLY

Adding custom code requires caution. Keep the embeds concise and well-tested, as a single misconfiguration can impact performance or break user flows. Whenever possible, host external scripts securely and integrate them via HTTPS. Document any changes you make so collaborators know how the snippet works, where it's deployed, and how to update or troubleshoot it if something goes wrong.

51.3 ENSURING COMPATIBILITY AND RESPONSIVENESS

Create a staging area before finalizing embedded scripts in production. Test thoroughly on multiple devices and screen sizes to confirm your code seamlessly scales with Adalo's responsive design. Watch for conflicts between your custom embed and Adalo's own libraries. If needed, reorder loading sequences or limit code execution to relevant screens, safeguarding the rest of your app from unintended side effects.

51.4 MAINTAINING AND EVOLVING EMBEDDED SOLUTIONS

As Adalo evolves, so too should your embedded code. Set reminders to review older snippets for compatibility, efficiency, or improved methods. Update libraries, fix deprecated functions, and keep an eye on error logs that might reveal hidden issues. With a thoughtful maintenance plan, you can combine the best of Adalo's no-code environment with the power of targeted custom scripts.

Chapter 52: AI and Machine Learning Integrations

Artificial intelligence (AI) and machine learning (ML) offer opportunities to transform user experiences, automate complex tasks, and deliver predictive insights. By integrating AI services into your Adalo project, you can develop more sophisticated apps—whether it's real-time language translation, intelligent recommendations, or automated data classification.

52.1 IDENTIFYING AI USE CASES

Pinpointing the right AI or ML overlap starts with a clear user benefit. You might analyze user actions to suggest products, conduct sentiment analysis on text inputs, or auto-tag images uploaded by the community. Aim for specific features that solve an evident user pain point, ensuring any added complexity is worthwhile.

52.2 CONNECTING THIRD-PARTY AI SERVICES

Services like Google Cloud AI, IBM Watson, or OpenAI provide ready-made ML models for speech, vision, text, and more. Use Adalo's external collections or custom workflows to interact with these APIs. Send data—like text snippets or image URLs—to the model, then store and display the returned intelligence in your app. Keep security in mind by properly safeguarding any API credentials and sensitive data.

52.3 TRAINING CUSTOM MODELS

If your app operates in a unique industry, off-the-shelf AI services may not suffice. Training custom models can yield specialized outputs—like analyzing niche terminologies or detecting anomalies in specific data sets. You'll likely use a separate ML platform to configure and refine the model, then hook it into Adalo with an API endpoint for inference. This approach demands more technical know-how but can differentiate your product with tailor-made intelligence.

52.4 BALANCING AI AUTOMATION AND USER CONTROL

Automating tasks without user oversight can yield confusion or mistrust—especially if an AI-driven feature makes unexpected decisions. Offer clear explanations about how your AI works and provide override options. This is particularly relevant for areas like automated moderation or heavy personalization. Striking a human-centric balance fosters transparency and confidence in your AI-powered components.

Chapter 53: Showcasing Your Portfolio

Whether you're a solo creator, part of a development team, or running an agency, displaying your Adalo accomplishments effectively can open doors to new clients and collaborations. A well-crafted portfolio highlights your expertise in designing intuitive interfaces, configuring data relationships, and delivering functional solutions that solve real-world problems.

53.1 SELECTING APPS TO FEATURE

Pick projects that showcase diverse skill sets—like an e-commerce platform with extensive payment flows, a social network with custom chat features, or a data-driven dashboard for enterprise clients. Demonstrating a broad range of capabilities convinces potential customers you can meet varied needs. If you have personal passion projects, include them to underscore your creativity and flexibility.

53.2 TELLING THE PROJECT STORY

A portfolio is more than screenshots. Describe each project's mission, your role, challenges encountered, and the results. Include a brief overview of how Adalo's features enabled you to innovate efficiently. Share insights into the design decisions that shaped the user experience or data flows. This narrative-driven approach paints a vivid picture of your problem-solving methodology.

53.3 CREATING ENGAGING VISUALS AND DEMOS

High-quality visuals—like short videos or animations of app interactions—help viewers grasp your work's impact quickly. Consider interactive prototypes that let them click through a simplified version of the user flow. By crafting a multimedia-rich portfolio, you grab and maintain attention, allowing your potential clients or employers to fully appreciate the artistry and structure behind your apps.

53.4 PROMOTING YOUR COLLECTION

Once your portfolio is ready, share it widely—on professional networks, in online communities, and via personal websites. Reach out to past clients for testimonials or case studies that reinforce your credibility. Continually update your collection as you refine skills, adopt new techniques, and complete more complex Adalo assignments. This constant refresh serves as a living testament to your growth.

Chapter 54: Industry-Specific Solutions

Adalo's versatile toolkit makes it adaptable to countless fields—from healthcare and education, to real estate and event management. Creating industry-specific solutions means tailoring your app's flows, features, and data structures to address the core pain points unique to each domain. By optimizing for specialized use cases, you position your products as indispensable tools within those markets.

54.1 HEALTHCARE AND TELEMEDICINE

Apps in healthcare involve patient records, appointment scheduling, and secure video consultations. Robust data privacy measures—like encryption and stringent access controls—are non-negotiable. Adalo's user roles and conditional logic can govern who sees appointment details or medical files. Integration with teleconferencing APIs can enable real-time checkups, turning your Adalo solution into a virtual clinic.

54.2 EDUCATION AND E-LEARNING

Educational platforms require course organization, progress tracking, and interactive quizzes or forums. By linking collections of lessons, tests, and user progress, you can build personalized dashboards for each student. Automated notifications remind learners of upcoming deadlines or newly unlocked materials. Incorporate multimedia elements for a richer experience, and let teachers analyze performance stats to adapt lessons more effectively.

54.3 REAL ESTATE AND PROPERTY MANAGEMENT

Property listings and rental tools hinge on intuitive data displays—users need to filter by location, price range, or property type. Adalo's lists combined with advanced filtering can power a robust search section. Include modules for scheduling viewings, managing tenancy agreements, and collecting rent via integrated payment gateways. This streamlined approach offers a one-stop management platform for buyers, sellers, and landlords alike.

54.4 EVENTS AND TICKETING SERVICES

Adalo's e-commerce and user authentication capabilities are well-suited for event management. Set up dynamic ticket pricing, seat selection, and automated confirmations to simplify attendance tracking. You can store specialized information such as QR codes or scannable passes within user profiles, ensuring a contactless entry experience. Add group chat or push notifications to keep attendees updated on schedule changes, speaker announcements, or special offers.

54.5 BUILDING NICHE SOLUTIONS

Whether it's custom CRM for local businesses or applications catering to hobby communities, find the unique pain points each industry segment faces. Use Adalo's flexibility to craft targeted data structures, focus on specialized workflows, and add integrations that directly support those use cases. Building niche solutions can position you as an industry leader, offering curated functionality that generic platforms might overlook.

www.ingramcontent.com/pod-product-compliance
Lightning Source LLC
LaVergne TN
LVHW051744050326
832903LV00029B/2709